Hide & ROCK PAINTING

hinkler

About This Book

This book contains everything you need to know to create beautiful and unique rock paintings. It also suggests excellent ways to display or play games with these rocks, like Painted-rock Hide-and-Seek.

To Make Great Rock Paintings You Will Need:

- Rocks of various shapes and sizes
- Paints (you will need all primary colours plus black and white)
- Paint brushes with both flat and round bristles
- Chalk
- Paint mixing tray
- Old jar (for water for your brushes)
- Felt
- Pencil
- Masking tape
- Sticky tape
- Old newspaper
- Large bull clip
- Paint pens
- Felt-tip pen

Published by Hinkler Books Pty Ltd
45–55 Fairchild Street
Heatherton Victoria 3202 Australia
www.hinkler.com

© Hinkler Books Pty Ltd 2013, 2017

Written by Jaclyn Crupi and Hinkler Studio
Cover photography by Ned Meldrum
Images © Shutterstock.com or Hinkler Books Pty Ltd

All rights reserved. No part of this publication may be reproduced, stored in a retrieval system, or transmitted in any way or by any means, electronic, mechanical, photocopying, recording or otherwise, without the prior written permission of Hinkler Books Pty Ltd.

ISBN: 978 1 4889 1063 0

Printed and bound in China

Contents

Getting started 4–5

Rock-painting Techniques 6–7

Playing Painted-rock Hide-and-Seek 8–11

Lovely Ladybird 12–13

Terrific Turtle 14–15

Flashy Fish 16–17

Cute Caterpillar 18–19

Buzzing Bee 20–21

Outstanding Owl 22–23

Perfect Panda 24–25

Ghostly Ghoul 26–27

Jazzy Jack-o'-Lantern 28–29

Spooky Spider 30–31

Super Santa 32–33

Radical Reindeer 34–35

Excellent Easter Egg 36–37

Wonderful Watermelon 38–39

Cute Cupcake 40–41

Perfect Pizza 42–43

Special Strawberry 44–45

More Painting Ideas 46–47

Further Rock Fun 48

Getting Started

Rock painting is a lot of fun, but before you can jump in, there are some basic things you need to do to get everything ready.

Find Rocks to Work With

Do you sometimes get home from a walk or the beach with pockets full of rocks? Are there rocks scattered all over your bedroom? Yes? Then you've got lots of material to work with already!

Choose Carefully

It's important to choose the right rock for your planned design. Rocks come in lots of shapes and sizes and some are better for certain designs than others. Imagine how your sketch will look on the rock before you begin. If it doesn't work with the rock shape, choose another rock.

Set Up

Have your palette and all your paints, brushes and other materials ready before you start. You don't want to have to stop to find materials once you've started painting.

Outdoor Paint

If any of your rock painting creations are intended to live outdoors, make sure you use outdoor paint. It would be such a shame if all your hard work washed away in the next rainstorm! Outdoor craft paint can be bought from most craft stores.

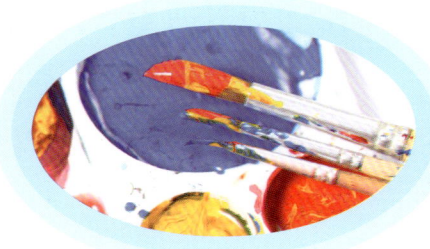

Top Tip
Painted rocks make great paperweights. To add a unique twist, use magnetic paint – then your rocks can also be used to hold paperclips!

Top Tip
Thin rocks can be placed in a bull clip and held so you can paint both sides of the rock. There's no time wasted waiting for one side to dry!

Clean and Tidy

Painting can be messy, so make sure you always cover your work area with old newspaper and have an old cloth on hand to wipe up any paint spills. Wear an apron or old shirt to protect your clothes.

Rock-Painting Techniques

It takes some planning and creativity to create rock paintings. Follow these simple techniques to make sure your rocks look fantastic and draw attention.

Sketch First

Always sketch out your idea before you lift a paintbrush. It's easier to picture what the finished project will look like if you draw it first with pencil on paper. You can then refer back to your sketch as you paint to help you stay on track.

The Right Brush for the Right Job

There are different sizes and types of paintbrushes, and each paintbrush is useful in different ways. Fine paintbrushes with round ends are good for decorations, details, outlines and final touches. Larger flat paintbrushes are good for backgrounds, blends and flat washes.

Dry, Dry, Dry

Make sure you allow the rock to dry between each coat of paint and each newly painted detail. It's very easy to smudge wet paint. If it's a sunny day, leave the rock to dry in the sun. Always paint one side of the rock and allow it to dry before turning it to paint the other side.

Colour Mixing

Primary colours are colours that no other colour combination can produce. From the three primary colours – red, blue and yellow – it's possible to make nearly any colour. This means that you only really need these colour paints, plus white and black, for your rock painting. Here's a guide to simple colour mixing.

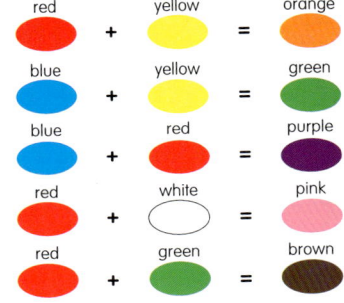

red + yellow = orange
blue + yellow = green
blue + red = purple
red + white = pink
red + green = brown

Finishing Spray

To protect your painted rock creations you can paint or spray a gloss (shiny) or matte (no shine) sealant on top. You can buy sealant from most craft stores.

Caring for Your Brushes

Follow these simple rules of caring for your paintbrushes.
- Always clean your brushes between colour changes.
- Never allow paint to dry on your brushes.
- Never let a brush sit in water. Clean or rinse your brushes and remove them from the water container. When the painting session is finished, clean all your brushes.
- Dry the brushes and reshape them with your fingers.
- Store your paintbrushes either lying flat or with the brush end upright.

Playing Painted-Rock Hide-and-seek

What better way to make the most of your awesome rock-art creations than by using them to play painted-rock hide-and-seek? This exciting game is becoming a global phenomenon and it's easy to see why: it's simple but super fun to play and can be enjoyed by a large group of people. Learn how you can join in the fun by following the instructions below.

The Aim of the Game

There are two sides to the game (just as there is in normal hide-and-seek): the first is to hide your painted rocks for people to find; the second is to find rocks that have been hidden by other people.

Private or Public Games

This game can be played at home or somewhere public, like a park, with friends and family. It makes a perfect party game!

You can also extend this game to wider painted-rock hide-and-seek communities. The best way to be involved in the larger community game is to ask your parents or guardians to find some of the social-media groups dedicated to this game. These groups will often list the different locations in your area where hidden rocks can be found, so you can find a location to play that's convenient for you.

When searching for online groups, note that the game is also referred to as 'painted-rock hunting'. Groups may allow you to record the general areas where you have hidden rocks (don't be too specific – it takes away the fun!), as well as to post pictures of your rocks and any clues that you want to give to their location. You can also post when you find other people's rocks, where and what they were. See 'Finding Rocks' on page 11 for more details.

Hiding Rocks

To participate in the hiding part of the game, first create an awesome piece of rock art on one side of the rock (this is the side that will face up). Instead of painting a cute picture, you may want to write a positive message, like 'Peace!' or 'You Rock!' – something uplifting and inspiring that you would like to find yourself. If you're playing a private game of rock hide-and-seek, you can paint the other side in a matching design.

9

If you're playing with the wider rock-finding community, you can write instructions on the back of the rock that tell the finder what social-media platform they should post a photo of the rock on when they find it. Include any group name, hashtag or web address used by your rock-hiding group, to make it super easy to follow. Make sure you leave enough space to fit all the words in! You might find it easier to write in permanent marker rather than painting the words. You can also post a photo of your rock to your social-media group, giving clues to where it's hidden.

TOP TIP
It's essential that you seal your rock's artwork before you play this game, because it needs to be able to survive getting wet and dirty.

Now it's time to hide that rock! Popular places to hide rocks include parks, playgrounds and walking trails. However, please be mindful of the area and the communities that use it. Don't hide rocks on private property! Some public places have restrictions and guidelines too – rock hide-and-seek is often not allowed in national parks, for example. If you aren't sure, ask a parent or guardian to look up the guidelines for that particular public space.

Finding Rocks

As well as hiding your own rocks, you can search for rocks that other people have hidden. When you find one, if it's part of a public game, you can then post a photo and message about finding the rock online, following the instructions recorded on the back of the rock. You can then either re-hide the rock in the same spot for others to find, hide it somewhere else (making sure you let the group know it's been re-hidden elsewhere), or keep it.

Please note:

It's very important to get the permission of your parents or guardians before going to public places to painted-rock hide-and-seek and before posting any pictures to social media. Always have an adult with you when playing this game in public places.

To Keep Or Not to Keep

It's more in the spirit of the game to take a photo of your victorious rock-finding moment and then re-hide the rock for others to find, rather than to keep the rock. A good compromise is to keep the first rock that you find, but make another one to replace it, and then to re-hide or replace all the other rocks that you find.

Lovely Ladybird

Ladybirds are fun and easy to paint on rocks, and look great. A few of them placed in the garden look wonderful and brighten things up nicely. They also make sweet gifts for family or friends.

You Will Need:

- Red, black, blue and white paint
- A small round or oval rock
- A medium flat brush
- A small flat brush
- A small round brush
- Chalk
- Pencil
- Paper
- Felt circles (optional)

How to Paint a Ladybird

1 Select a rock. Small round or oval rocks are the best shape for ladybirds.

2 Paint the rock with a basecoat of white with a medium flat brush. Colours such as red or yellow look best and are brighter when painted on a white basecoat.

3 Once the white has dried, paint the rock red all over. You might need to give the rock two or three coats of red before you have solid coverage.

4 Sketch out a ladybird design on paper.

5 Refer to your sketch and use chalk to map out the area for the head, then draw a line down the centre of the body.

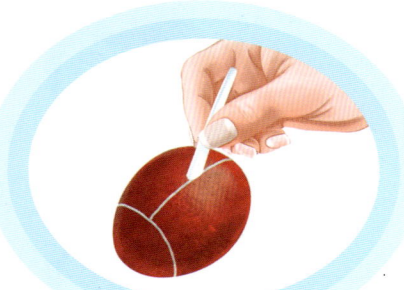

TOP TIP
You don't have to use red as your base colour for ladybirds. Yellow, pink, blue and even purple look good, too.

6 Paint the head black with the small flat brush. Paint the line down the body black with the small round brush.

7 Add black dots to the body. You can do this with a round brush or dip your finger in black paint and apply to the body. You could also use the base of a pen or pencil as a round stamp to apply the black paint dots.

8 With chalk, draw a line down the centre of the face, dividing it in half. This will help you evenly draw in the eyes, nose and mouth. Use the chalk to draw a mouth.

9 To draw the eye outlines use a pencil, as chalk is too thick. You can outline felt circles or create circle templates by cutting circles out of thick paper. This will ensure your ladybird eyes are perfectly and evenly round.

10 Paint the inside of the eyes white with a small round brush. You might need to do more than one coat.

11 Paint two white nostril holes on either side of the chalk line running down the middle of the face.

12 Paint the chalk mouth line white with the small round brush or the thinnest brush you have.

13 Paint a smaller black circle inside each eye. You can use small felt circles or handmade circle templates to help with this.

14 Paint a small white dot within the black circles with the small round brush. Paint a blue outline around each black circle, slightly thicker at the top than the bottom.

15 Paint over the white mouth line in red with the small round brush.

16 Paint thin white arches above each eye for the antennae.

17 When dry, your ladybird rock painting is finished!

13

Terrific Turtle

A turtle shell is the perfect image to paint onto a rock. In this design, craft sticks form the turtle's legs and face and the painted rock is used to make the shell.

You will need:

- Green, black and brown paint
- A medium oval or round rock
- A medium flat brush
- A small flat brush
- A small round brush
- Chalk
- Pencil
- Paper
- 2 small googly eyes
- 3 craft sticks, 1 complete and 2 broken in half
- Craft or cement glue (ask an adult for help if using cement glue)

How to Paint a Turtle

1. Select a rock. Medium round or oval rocks are the best shape for turtle shells.

2. Paint the rock with green paint all over using a medium flat brush. If your green paint is too bright, mix it with some blue paint. You might need to give the rock two or three coats before you have solid coverage.

3. Paint the craft sticks all over using the same green paint and medium flat brush.

4. Sketch out a turtle shell design on paper.

5 Refer to your sketch and map out the sections of the turtle's shell on the rock using chalk.

6 Use craft glue to stick the four craft stick pieces to the complete craft stick as shown.

7 Use craft glue to stick the googly eyes to the top of the complete craft stick.

8 Paint the chalk shell outlines black with a small round brush.

9 Using the brown paint and the small flat brush, fill in the sections of the shell.

10 Glue the painted rock to the painted craft stick legs and face. Be sure to ask an adult for help if using cement glue.

11 When dry, your turtle rock painting is finished!

TOP TIP
Instead of using craft sticks for the turtle's face and legs you could use five small rocks. Paint toes on four of them and eyes on one and glue them underneath your painted shell rock.

15

Flashy Fish

Clown fish are bright and attractive. They live in coral reefs. You're sure to find a rock perfectly shaped to make a great clown fish rock painting.

You Will Need:

- Orange, white and black paint
- A small flat rock with a peak at the top
- A medium flat brush
- A small flat brush
- A small round brush
- Chalk
- Pencil
- Paper

How to Paint a Clown Fish

1 Select a rock. Small flat rocks with a peak at the top are the best shape for clown fish.

2 Paint the rock with a basecoat of white using a medium flat brush. Colours such as orange and yellow look best and are brighter when painted on a white basecoat.

3 Paint the rock with bright orange paint all over. You might need to give the rock two or three coats before you have solid coverage. If you don't have orange paint, you can make it by mixing yellow and red paint. Start with yellow paint and add a small amount of red paint to it very slowly. You won't need much red paint.

4 Sketch out a clown fish design on paper.

5 Refer to your sketch and map out the sections for the white stripes and fin on the rock using chalk.

6 Paint the stripes white using a small flat brush. You might need to paint two or three coats.

7 Paint black outlines around the white stripes using the small round brush. Keep your hand steady. Add extra definition to the fin with black paint.

8 Use a small round brush to paint a black dot for the eye and a small smile for the mouth.

9 When dry, your clown fish rock painting is finished!

TOP TIP
Clown fish live in coral reefs. Paint some rocks with coral to place around your clown fish so it's in its environment. Starfish are also fun to paint on rocks!

Cute Caterpillar

A series of painted rocks lined up in a row make a great caterpillar. You can even glue all the rocks together!

You Will Need:

- A selection of colour paints
- Six or more similar-sized rocks
- A medium flat brush
- A small flat brush
- A small round brush
- Chalk
- Pencil
- Paper
- Craft or cement glue (optional – ask an adult for help if using cement glue)

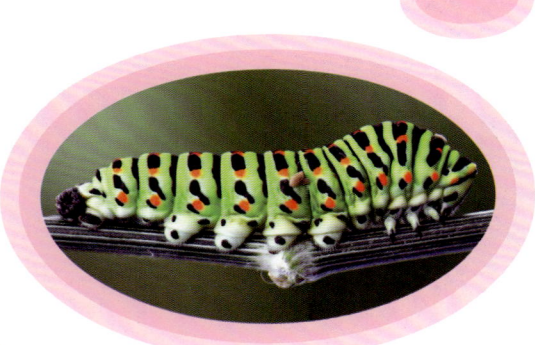

How to Paint a Caterpillar

1 Select six or more rocks. Make sure they are similar sizes but choose smaller ones for the head rock and final rock.

2 Paint the rocks with a basecoat of white using a medium flat brush. Many colours are brighter when painted on a white basecoat.

3 Paint each rock a different colour using a medium flat brush. Choose colours that complement each other.

4. Sketch out design patterns for each rock on paper. Choose a different design for each rock. Plan what colour paints you will use for the details on each rock.

5. Refer to your sketch and use a small round brush or flat brush to paint dots, stripes and any other kind of designs you sketched for each rock. Use the colour paints you used in your design.

6. Paint a face on the first rock.

7. Use a small round brush to paint little legs and feet on the sides of all the rocks except the head.

8. Place a large amount of glue between each rock and stick them together. Be sure to ask an adult for help if using cement glue.

9. When dry, your caterpillar rock painting is finished!

TOP TIP
Caterpillars turn into butterflies. Trace the butterfly design on page 48 and use it to paint a butterfly rock painting.

Buzzing Bee

Painted bee rocks look very cute and cheery. They are bright and happy and look great inside on a windowsill.

You Will Need:

- Yellow, black and white paint
- A round-, oval- or teardrop-shaped rock
- A medium flat brush
- A small round brush
- Chalk
- Pencil
- Paper

How to Paint a Bee

1. Select a rock. Round-, oval- or teardrop-shaped rocks are best for bees.

2. Paint the rock with a basecoat of white using a medium flat brush. Colours such as orange or yellow look best and are brighter when painted on a white basecoat.

3. Once the white has dried, paint the rock yellow all over with a flat brush. You might need to give the rock two or three coats of yellow before you have solid coverage.

4. Sketch out a bee design on paper.

5. Refer to your sketch and map out the stripes on the rock using chalk. You can make the stripes straight or wavy.

6 Paint over the chalk stripes with black paint using the small round brush. You can make the stripes as thick or as thin as you like.

7 With chalk, mark where each eye will go on the rock. Paint the eyes black using the small round brush. You can use the eraser end of a pencil to make the two eyes. Simply dip the eraser in black paint and stamp over the chalk circles. This will ensure your bee eyes are perfectly and evenly round.

8 Paint a white antenna above each eye with the small round brush. Keep a steady hand.

9 Using the small round brush, paint a black circle for the nose. Add a curved line for the mouth.

10 Add a small white dot to each eye. You can use the end of a thin paintbrush to do this.

11 Use chalk to sketch the wings onto the rock.

12 Use the small round brush to paint the outline of the wings in white paint.

13 When dry, your bee rock painting is finished!

TOP TIP

If you want to paint the bee's wings, dilute white paint with water to make it transparent. It needs to be thin enough that you can see the bee's yellow body through the paint. Use a small flat brush to lightly paint the outline of the wings.

Outstanding Owl

Owls are great subjects for rock paintings. You can make your painted owl rock look adorable by using pastel colours.

You Will Need:

- Green, beige, white, yellow and black paint
- An oval flat rock
- A medium flat brush
- A small flat brush
- A small round brush
- Chalk
- Pencil
- Paper

How to Paint an Owl

1 Select a rock. Oval rocks are the best shape for owls.

2 Paint the rock with a basecoat of white using a medium flat brush.

3 Once the white has dried, paint the rock beige all over with a small or medium flat brush. You might need to give the rock two or three coats of beige before you have solid coverage. If you don't have beige paint, mix some red and yellow paint and add a dash of blue. Mix a small amount of this with some white paint. Keep adding the colour mix until you have a warm beige colour.

4 Sketch out an owl design on paper.

22

5 Refer to your sketch and map out the outline of the owl's wings, body and face on the rock in chalk (use coloured chalk if it's hard to see white chalk on the beige).

6 Use the small flat brush to paint the wings light green. Lighten your green paint by adding some white paint. This makes a warmer pastel colour.

7 Use the small round brush to paint around the face with blue paint.

8 With the small round brush, paint large white ovals for the eyes.

9 With the small round brush paint a small yellow upside-down triangle shape for the nose.

10 With the end of a fine paintbrush paint small blue dots onto the owl's chest.

11 With the end of a fine paintbrush add a black dot to the inside of both eyes.

12 When dry, your owl rock painting is finished!

TOP TIP

You don't always have to paint the whole animal's body on the rock. You could just do the face. Owls have very interesting eyes so you could make this a focus of your rock painting.

Perfect Panda

Create a complete panda rock painting by stacking multiple rocks on top of each other. Each rock has a certain part of the panda's body painted on it. The result looks adorable.

You Will Need:

- Black, white and pink paint
- A large round rock with a flat bottom, an oval flat rock, two small black pebbles
- A medium flat brush
- A small flat brush
- A small round brush
- Chalk
- Pencil
- Paper
- Black felt tip pen
- Craft or cement glue (ask an adult for help if using cement glue)

How to Paint a Panda

1 Select your rocks. The large round rock will need to be able to rest securely on its flat bottom. The oval flat rock will be glued to the large round rock so make sure they connect. The two small black pebbles will be stuck to the flat rock for the panda's ears.

2 Paint the large round rock and the oval flat rock white using a medium flat brush. You might need to give the rocks two or three coats of white before you have solid coverage.

TOP TIP
Gluing rocks together can be tricky. In addition to cement glue, there are hot glues that will ensure your rocks remain stuck. Be sure to ask an adult for help with hot glues.

3 Sketch out a panda design for each rock on paper. The large rock is for the belly and needs to include the panda's arms and belly button. The oval flat rock is for the panda's face.

4 Refer to your sketch and use chalk to map out the outline of the panda's belly on the large rock.

5 Use the small flat brush to paint the panda's black arms and belly base.

6 Use a black felt tip pen or small round brush to add a belly button in black paint.

7 Refer to your sketch and use pencil to draw where the eyes, nose and mouth will go on the flat rock.

8 Using the small round brush, paint large black ovals for the eyes.

9 Using the small round brush, paint a small pink oval shape for the nose.

10 With the end of a fine paintbrush add a white dot to the inside of both eyes.

11 Use a black felt tip pen or small round brush to add a small smile.

12 Glue the oval flat rock to the large round rock. Be sure to ask an adult for help if using cement glue.

13 Glue the two small black pebbles to the oval flat rock as ears. Be sure to ask an adult for help if using cement glue.

14 When dry, your panda rock painting is finished!

Ghostly Ghoul

Did you ever think a rock could look scary? It will once you've painted this ghostly ghoul!

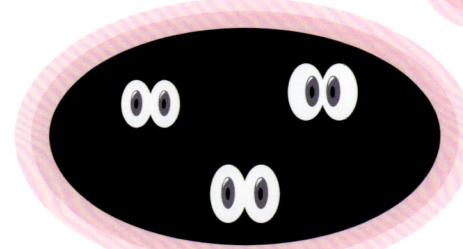

You will need:

- Black, white and bright green paint
- A large flat rock
- A medium flat brush
- A small flat brush
- A small round brush
- Chalk
- Pencil
- Paper
- Black felt tip pen

How to Paint a Ghost

1 Select your rock. A large flat rock works best for painting a ghoulish ghost.

2 Paint the rock white using a medium flat brush. This is a basecoat and will make sure the bright green is as bright and ghoulish as possible.

3 Paint the rock green all over using a medium flat brush. Apply a second green coat so the colour is really bright.

4 Sketch out a ghost design on paper. Look at the ghost faces on the next page for some ideas for extra detail.

5 Refer to your sketch and use chalk to map out the outline of the ghost on the rock.

6 With the small flat brush, paint the interior of the ghost white.

7 Use the small round brush to outline the ghost in black paint. This needs a steady hand, so take your time.

8 Use the small round brush to paint in the black dots for eyes and an open mouth. Use a black felt tip pen if your face design is more detailed.

9 When dry, your ghost rock painting is finished!

TOP TIP
You can paint large heavy rocks as simple ghosts. The unusual shapes of these rocks look really good as ghosts. Paint the whole rock white (two coats should be enough) and then paint two black oval eyes and a black round nose on the front of the rock. Simple and fun!

Some ghost face design ideas.

Jazzy Jack-o'-Lantern

Painted rocks make great Halloween decorations. Round flat rocks are the perfect shape for jack-o'-lanterns. It looks great to have several of these grouped together, all with slightly different facial expressions.

You Will Need:

- Orange, black, white and green paint
- An oval or round flat rock
- A medium flat brush
- A small round brush
- Chalk
- Pencil
- Paper

How to Paint a Jack-o'-Lantern

1. Select your rock. A flat oval or round rock works best for painting a jack-o'-lantern.
2. Paint the rock with a basecoat of white using a medium flat brush.
3. Paint the rock orange all over using a medium flat brush. Apply a second orange coat so the colour is bright and you have good coverage. If you don't have orange paint, you can make it by mixing yellow and red paint. Start with yellow paint and add red to it very slowly. You won't need much red paint.

4 Sketch out a jack-o'-lantern design on paper. Look at the jack-o'-lantern faces at the bottom of these pages for some ideas for extra detail.

5 Refer to your sketch and use chalk to map out the outline of the jack-o'-lantern on the rock.

6 Using the small round brush paint the jack-o'-lantern's eyes, nose and mouth with black paint.

TOP TIP

Can't choose which expression to use? Don't just make one jack-o'-lantern rock painting, make 10! These rocks look great when there are lots of them, all with different features and expressions.

7 Use the small round brush to paint a small green stem at the top.

8 When dry, your jack-o'-lantern rock painting is finished!

Some jack-o'-lantern design ideas.

Spooky Spider

Having a spooky spider rock painting on your window ledge is much cuter than having a real spider! The black pipe cleaners form the spider's hairy legs and the painted rock is the spider's body.

You will need:

- Black, grey and white paint
- An oval or round rock
- A medium flat brush
- A small round brush
- Chalk
- Pencil
- Paper
- 4 black pipe cleaners
- Craft glue

How to Paint a Spider

1 Select your rock. An oval or round rock works best for painting a spider.

2 Paint the rock with a basecoat of white using a medium flat brush.

3 Paint the rock black all over using a medium flat brush. Apply a second black coat so you have good coverage.

4 Sketch out a design on paper for the face of your spider.

5 Refer to your sketch and use chalk to map out where the eyes and mouth are to go on the rock.

6 You can add hairy detail to the spider's body using a small round brush and grey paint.

7 Fold each black pipe cleaner in half. Glue two folded pipe cleaners on the bottom of each side of the rock to form the spider's eight legs.

8 Using the small round brush paint the spider's mouth with white paint.

9 Using the small round brush paint the eyes white. When dry, add a small black dot to each eye.

10 When dry, your spider rock painting is finished!

TOP TIP
Why not paint another rock with a spider web to sit next to your spooky spider rock painting?

Super Santa

Rock paintings make unique and special Christmas decorations. Round and oval rocks work best for Santa's face. The longer the rock, the bushier Santa's beard will be!

You Will Need:

- Black, white, red, blue and pink paint
- An oval or round flat rock
- A medium flat brush
- A small round brush
- Chalk (coloured)
- Pencil
- Paper
- Black paint pen or felt tip pen
- Glitter

How to Paint Santa

1. Select your rock. A flat oval or round rock works best for painting a Santa face.

2. Paint the rock with a basecoat of white using a medium flat brush.

3. Paint another coat of white all over the rock using a medium flat brush.

4. Sketch out a Santa face design on paper. Look at the Santa face here for an idea of the features you could include.

5 Refer to your sketch and use coloured chalk or pencil to map out the outline of Santa's hat, beard, eyes, nose and mouth on the rock.

6 Paint Santa's hat red using the medium flat brush.

7 Use the small round brush to outline the white sections of Santa's hat with black paint. For a finer line use a paint pen or felt tip pen.

8 Use the small round brush to paint Santa's face a skin tone. Mix pink paint with white paint until you have a natural skin colour.

9 Use the small round brush to outline Santa's nose, eyes and mouth with black paint. For a finer line use a paint pen or felt tip pen.

10 Use the small round brush to fill in Santa's eyebrows, eyes and moustache with white paint. Using the same brush, add some red paint to Santa's mouth and cheeks.

11 Use the small round brush to add some texture and detail to Santa's white beard. You could add some tone by mixing a small amount of blue paint in with some white paint and painting long stripes down Santa's beard area.

12 While the paint is still wet, sprinkle some glitter onto Santa's beard. It will stick to the paint and add sparkle.

13 When dry, your Santa rock painting is finished!

TOP TIP
Glue a looped ribbon to the top of your painted rock and hang it on your Christmas tree as a new and unique ornament!

Radical Reindeer

It's up to you whether or not you give your reindeer a red nose. You could even create a rock painting for each of Santa's reindeer – Dasher, Dancer, Prancer, Vixen, Comet, Cupid, Donner, Blitzen and Rudolph, of course!

You Will Need:

- Black, white, brown and red paint
- A slightly oval flat rock
- A medium flat brush
- A small round brush
- Chalk
- Pencil
- Paper
- 2 twigs (optional)

How to Paint a Reindeer

1. Select your rock. A slightly oval rock works best for painting a reindeer head.

2. Paint the rock with a basecoat of white using a medium flat brush.

3. Paint a coat of brown all over the rock using a medium flat brush. Apply a second coat to ensure you have good coverage.

4. Sketch out a reindeer face design on paper. One option is to make the head section round with a small oval overlapping at the bottom of it. Two pointy ears on either side of the head and the antlers are all that need to be added (if you're not using twigs for antlers).

5. Refer to your sketch and use chalk to map out the outline of the reindeer's face on the rock. It might make it easier to think of the shapes within the design.

6 Use the small round brush to paint the chalked face outline in white on the rock.

7 Use the small round brush to paint the eyes.

8 With the end of a fine paintbrush add a black dot to the inside of both eyes.

9 Use the small round brush to paint the ears black.

10 Use the small round brush to paint the reindeer's nose red (optional).

11 If using, glue the twigs to the top of the rock at the back to act as the antlers.

12 When dry, your reindeer rock painting is finished!

TOP TIP
You can add fine texture to the reindeer's fur with a liner brush and some white paint. Make sure you follow the direction of the fur and paint small white lines.

Excellent Easter Egg

In addition to painting real eggs, painted rock eggs make lovely Easter decorations. You can even use them in your Easter egg hunt along with the chocolate ones!

You Will Need:

- A selection of pastel-coloured paints or metallic paint if you have it
- White paint
- An oval rock
- A medium flat brush
- A small round brush
- Chalk
- Pencil
- Paper
- Glitter

How to Paint an Easter Egg

1 Select your rock. An oval-shaped rock works best for painting an Easter egg.

2 Paint the rock with a basecoat of white using a medium flat brush.

3 Paint the rock a pastel colour all over using a medium flat brush. Apply a second coat so you have good coverage. If you don't have any pastel-coloured paints you can lighten your bright colour paints by adding white or yellow paint. Metallic paint also looks good if you have it.

4 Sketch out an Easter pattern on paper. Look at the patterns below for inspiration. You can use a combination of dots, zigzags and stripes, for example.

5 You can either treat the entire rock as the egg or paint an outline of an egg onto one side of the rock. Both look festive so it's up to you. Refer to your sketch and use chalk to map out the outline of the Easter patterns on the rock.

6 If you have chosen to outline the egg on the rock, use the small round brush to paint the outline of the egg in white.

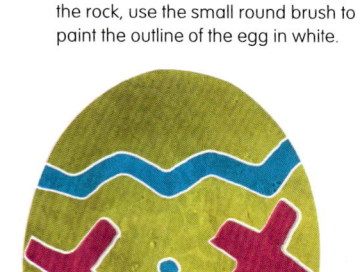

7 With the small round brush, paint the patterns onto the rock, using different-coloured paints for each pattern. Use the end of a fine paintbrush dipped in paint to add any dots.

8 When dry, your Easter egg rock painting is finished!

TOP TIP
A collection of painted rock Easter eggs look great in a cane basket full of straw (use shredded paper if you don't have any straw).

Some patterns for you to use as inspiration when painting your rock Easter egg.

Wonderful Watermelon

There's something particularly cute about rocks painted as food. Some rocks are perfectly shaped watermelon slices – look out for them for this design.

You Will Need:

- Red, black, white and green paint
- A curved triangular-shaped rock
- A medium flat brush
- A small round brush
- Chalk
- Pencil
- Paper

How to Paint a Watermelon

1 Select your rock. A curved triangular-shaped flat rock works best for painting a watermelon slice.

2 Paint the rock with a basecoat of white using a medium flat brush. Colours such as red or yellow look best and are brighter when painted on a white basecoat.

3 Once the white has dried, paint the rock red all over. You might need to give the rock two or three coats of red before you have solid coverage.

4 Sketch out a watermelon slice design on paper.

5 Refer to your sketch and use chalk to map out on the rock the sections for the red part of the fruit and the green rind. Think about how you want to place the seeds – scattered or in an arc.

6 Use the medium flat brush to paint the rind section green. This might take two coats to get good coverage.

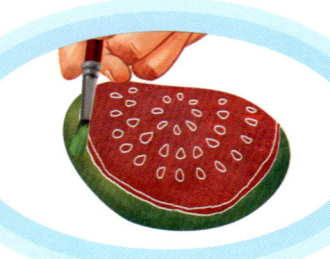

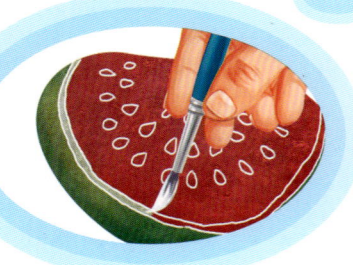

7 Use the small round brush to paint a white line to separate the red section from the green rind. Add some wiggly white lines to the green rind section using the small round brush.

8 Paint teardrop-shaped seeds onto the red section as designed in your sketch. The seeds can be black, white or a combination. If teardrop shapes are too hard to create, just dab the paint on with your brush.

9 When dry, your watermelon rock painting is finished!

TOP TIP

As you get more confident painting on rocks you can think more about ways to add texture and detail to your paintings. You can also experiment with colour mixing to create a whole new palette for your rock painting creations.

Cute Cupcake

Everyone loves cupcakes. But make sure you don't bite into this rock art creation – you might break a tooth!

You will need:

- A selection of pastel-coloured paints
- A large round arched rock
- A medium flat brush
- A small round brush
- Chalk
- Pencil
- Paper

How to Paint a Cupcake

1. Select your rock. A large arch-topped rock works best for painting a cupcake. Try to find a rock that's about the size of an actual cupcake.

2. Paint the rock with a basecoat of white using a medium flat brush. Pastel colours look best and are brighter when painted on a white basecoat.

3. Sketch out a cupcake design on paper. Does your cupcake have a liner? If so, what colour is it? Does it have a pattern on it? Then think about the cupcake. What colour is the icing? Are there sprinkles? A cherry?

4 Once the white has dried, paint a pastel colour of your choice all over. This should be the colour of your cupcake liner or the colour of the cupcake – yellow for vanilla or brown for chocolate. You might need to give the rock two or three coats before you have solid coverage.

5 Refer to your design and sketch the cupcake shape onto the rock using chalk. Show where the various toppings and decorations are to be painted.

6 Use the medium flat brush to paint the icing colour onto the top section of the rock.

TOP TIP
Use a hole puncher to punch small circles of coloured paper. Sprinkle these on top of your cupcake before the icing paint dries. The coloured paper will look like round sprinkles.

7 Use the small round brush to paint on all the toppings and decorations.

8 When dry, your cupcake rock painting is finished!

Perfect Pizza

Transform a rock into a piping-hot slice of pizza. All you have to do is find the right shape rock and choose your toppings.

You will need:

- White, brown, green, red, black and yellow paint
- A flat triangular (isosceles) rock
- A medium flat brush
- A small round brush
- Chalk
- Pencil
- Paper

How to Paint a Pizza Slice

1. Select your rock. Think about a slice of pizza. It's an isosceles triangle shape, with two long sides and one short side (the crust).

2. Paint the rock with a basecoat of white using a medium flat brush.

3. Sketch out a pizza slice design on paper. Think about the toppings. Are there mushrooms? Ham? Black olives? Tomatoes?

4 Use chalk to sketch out where the crust is and where you want to place your various toppings on the rock.

5 Use the medium flat brush to paint a light-brown colour for the crust section. Add some white paint to your brown paint if it's too dark.

6 Use your small round brush to paint your toppings. Try to make your paintings look like the vegetable or meat you're painting.

7 Use the small round brush to add some yellow sections for the melted cheese.

8 Use the small round brush to paint a brown outline around the toppings section of the rock. This adds definition to the rock.

9 When dry, your pizza slice rock painting is finished!

TOP TIP
Once you've mastered painting pizza-slice rocks, your next challenge is painting a hamburger rock. Find a rock that's the shape of a hamburger and focus on the coloured layers of filling on the side.

Special Strawberry

Fresh strawberries are delicious in summer. With these rock paintings you'll be able to look at fresh strawberries all year round.

You Will Need:

- White, red, green and black paint
- A small oval rock
- A medium flat brush
- A small round brush
- A liner brush
- Chalk
- Pencil
- Paper

How to Paint a Strawberry

1 Select a rock. Small oval-shaped rocks are the best shape for strawberries. Try to find a rock that is about the same size and shape as a strawberry.

2 Paint the rock with a basecoat of white using a medium flat brush. Colours such as red look best and are brighter when painted on a white basecoat.

3 Once the white has dried, paint the rock red all over. You might need to give the rock two or three coats of red before you have solid coverage.

4 Sketch out a strawberry design on paper.

5 Refer to your sketch and use chalk to map out on the rock the section for the green hull. Place the hull on the less pointed end of the rock.

6 Use your small round brush to paint the green hull and leaves.

7 With your small round brush, use a darker green paint (add black to your green paint to darken it) to paint an outline around the hull and leaves. Add some texture and details to the leaves.

8 Use a small round brush to add small black lines for the strawberry seeds to the red section of the rock.

TOP TIP
It's easy to adapt these instructions to make pineapple rock paintings.

9 Use a liner brush to add tiny white dots to the black seed lines.

10 When dry, your strawberry rock painting is finished!

45

More Painting Ideas

The only limit to what you can paint on rocks is your imagination. Don't feel you always have to paint specific objects – get your paints and rocks out and see what happens.

Words

Personalise a rock-painting gift with words. Two rocks painted with the words 'Best Friends' make a lovely gift. You can also paint single letters on each rock to spell out words such as 'Home', 'Garden' or a person's name. Your unique and personal creation is sure to be appreciated.

Graffiti-inspired lettering looks great on rocks.

A row of rocks all painted with bunting looks gorgeous and is a great gift when a baby is born.

Patterns

Patterns look great painted on rocks. Create your own patterns and have fun painting them. If the end result turns out differently to what you had in mind that's okay. It's fun to just relax and paint patterns using different colours. When grouped together, patterned rocks make great decorations on windowsills or in the garden.

Rock Monsters

Painting rock monsters is lots of fun. Make rock monsters for your friends. Just paint rocks different colours and paint funny monster mouths and teeth on each. Add crazy eyes, or glue on googly ones, and they're ready to give away.

Let the Rock Decide

Sometimes the shape of a rock will bring an object to mind. This makes it a perfect rock to paint that object on! It's already the right shape and has already made you think of something specific.

Your Creations

Rock painting is a fun and relaxing creative hobby. The results are unique and handmade by YOU! Be sure to add your initials to the backs (or bottoms) of your rock painting creations and the year you painted them.

Further Rock Fun

There are lots of fantastic and creative uses for your painted rocks. You can create your own rock pets and rock families – try out different kooky characters and animals! Painted rocks are great for decorating your desk or backyard, and they make awesome presents for your friends and family. Your rock creations can also be used as game pieces for boardgames or for playing your own version of the classic game noughts and crosses (e.g. with strawberries and bees instead of noughts and crosses!). What creative new uses for your rock art can you come up with?